8/13

# Paul Gauguin

Illustrated by Jean-Philippe C
Created by Frédéric Sorbier,
Jean-Philippe Chabot
and Gallimard Jeunesse

MOONLIGHT / FIRST DISCOVERY / ART

Aged forty,
Paul Gaugin
said he
wanted to
be a child.

So, he decided
to become a painter,
and to do
drawings
like a child.

For fun he painted
3 puppies lapping up
milk from a large
saucepan in the
middle of a table.

Then
3 glasses and
3 little apples.

In this picture
everything is round
like the number 3.

Gaugin
left Paris
for the country
in Britanny.

The clean lines
and vivid colours
of Japanese art fascinated him,

For him, Britanny
was as exotic
as Japan.

He escaped from the noisy stress  of a modern city...

Gaugin imagined the story in the Bible of Jacob wrestling with the angel but on red grass.

The faces and dresses of the women stand out like the pieces of a jigsaw.

Gaugin found that Britanny was not far enough away for him to feel as free as a "savage".
He took a boat to the other end of the world, to the Island of Tahiti in the Pacific Ocean.

The island
is like
paradise.

There nature is  kind
and generous.
All you have to do is
stretch out your hand
and pick fruit
like these red bananas.

Gaugin liked these bright colours.

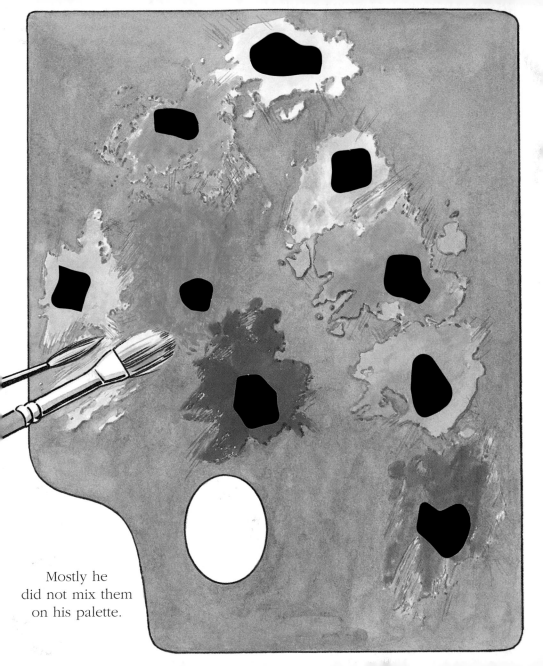

Mostly he
did not mix them
on his palette.

When young
painters asked
for advice
he told them:

pineapple

apple

lemon

blueberry

hazelnut

banana

mandarine

papaya

kiwi fruit

*" How do you see the
shadows? as blues?
Then paint them with the
purest blue on your palette"*

They are not the true colours. Gaugin did not want to copy what he saw,
but to create what does not exist except in his paintings.

Gaugin lived in a beach hut
made of wood.
His "Tropical Studio"
took up most of the space.

Late in his life,
he brought together
all the subjects
of his old paintings
like a collage
on one gigantic canvas.

Women pick and eat fruit near the blue statue
of an Indian goddess.
Can you spot the dog, the kittens, the goat,
the goose and the brightly coloured bird?

It is a poetic picture about the joy of living, about birth and creation: There is a baby at one end and an old lady at the other.

And now let's look at some of
Gaugin's most beautiful paintings.

*Child dreaming*
1881

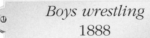

*Boys wrestling*
1888

*Seascape with Cow at the Edge of a Cliff* 1888

*Beautiful Angela*
1889

Gauguin was also a sculptor and carved many
native goddesses out of tree trunks
The "creator of the world"
is wearing a shell
above her head
like a halo.

*Goddess with a Shell*
1892

*Self-portrait with Palette*
1894

*The White Horse*
1898

*Bathers*
1902

Look at these details
of paintings
in this book
and see if you can
match them up.

Cover: **Paul Gauguin**, *Arearea*, 1892,
oil on canvas, 75 x 94 cm,
Musée d'Orsay. © RMN / G. Blot
Title page: *Self-portrait with Palette*, 1894, oil on
canvas, 92 x 73 cm, private coll., rights reserved
*Still Life with Three Puppies*, 1888,
oil on wood, 92 x 63 cm,
The Museum of Modern Art, New York,
Mrs. Simon Guggenheim Fund
© The Museum of Modern Art, New York, 1998


**Hokusai**, *study of wrestlers, extract from
Mangwa* (detail), Bibliotheque Nationale
**Hirishige**, *Plum Tree in Blossom*
print, 36.1 x 25.5 cm, J.Ostier Gallery, Paris
© Giraudon
**Emile Bernard**, *Breton Women in a Field*,
1888, oil on canvas, 74 x 92 cm,
private collection C. Giraudon.
© ADAGP. Paris, 1998
**Emile Bernard**, *Breton Women going to
Church*, 1892, oil on canvas, 75 x 100 cm
private coll. Musée Maurice Denis
*"le Prieué"* © ADAGP, Paris; 1998
**Paul Gauguin**, *Vision after the Sermon* or
*Jacob wrestling with the Angel*, 1888,
oil on canvas, 73 x 92 cm,
National Gallery of Scotland, Edinburgh
*The Meal* or *The Bananas*, oil on paper
with a canvas backing, 73 x 92 cm,
Musée d'Orsay. © RMN / H Lewandowski

*When will you marry?*, 1892, oil on canvas,
101.5 x 77.5 cm, Staechelin Collection, Basel
© Artothek / Artiphot / H. Hinz.
*Where do we come from? What are we?
Where are we going?*, 1897, oil on canvas
139 x 374.5 cm, Museum of Fine Arts,
Boston, Tompkins Collection.
© 1998 The Museum of Fine Arts, Boston.
*Child Dreaming*, 1881, oil on canvas,
59.5 x 73.5 cm. © Ordrupgaard,
Copenhagen / O. Woldbye
*Boys Wrestling*, 1888, oil on canvas,
93 x 73 cm, Josefowitz Collection
*Seascape with a Cow at the Edge of a Cliff*,
1888, oil on canvas, 73 x 60 cm
© Musée des Arts Décoratifs,
Paris / L. S. Jaulmes
*Beautiful Angela*, 1889, oil on canvas,
92 x 73 cm, Musée d'Orsay.
© RMN / J. Schormans
*Goddess with a Shell*, 1892
ironwood, mother of pearl and bone
27 x 14 cm, Musée d'Orsay
© RMN / H. Lewandowski
*Self-portrait with Palette*, 1894, oil on canvas,
92 x 73 cm, private collection, rights reserved
*The White Horse*, 1898, oil on canvas,
140 x 91 cm, Musée d'Orsay. © RMN/ G: Blot.
*Bathers*, 1902, oil on canvas, 92 x 73 cm,
Basil Goulandris Collection, Lausanne
rights reserved

Translator ; Penelope Stanley-Baker
ISBN 185103 357 2
© 1999 by Editions Gallimard Jeunesse
English text © 2005 by Moonlight Publishing Ltd

First published in the United Kingdom 2005
by Moonlight Publishing Ltd, The King's Manor,
East Hendred, Oxon OX12 8JY UK
Printed in Italy by Editoriale Lloyd